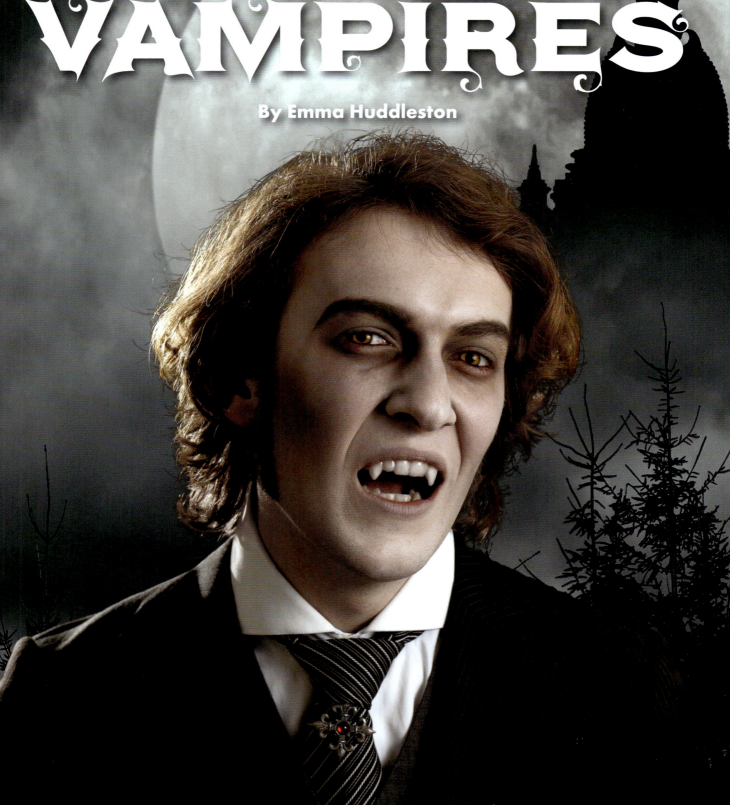

VAMPIRES

By Emma Huddleston

Published by The Child's World®
1980 Lookout Drive • Mankato, MN 56003-1705
800-599-READ • www.childsworld.com

Photographs ©: Alberto Gagna/iStockphoto, cover (vampire), 1 (vampire); Shutterstock Images, cover (background), 1–3 (background), 9, 13, 23, 24; Denis Tangney Jr./iStockphoto, 5; iStockphoto, 6–7, 8, 10, 16, 17; Red Line Editorial, 12; Kiselev Andrey Valerevich/Shutterstock Images, 15; Rob Cartorres/Shutterstock Images, 19; picture-alliance/Newscom, 20; World History Archive/Newscom, 21

Copyright © 2022 by The Child's World®
All rights reserved. No part of this book may be reproduced or utilized in any form or by any means without written permission from the publisher.

ISBN 9781503849785 (Reinforced Library Binding)
ISBN 9781503850842 (Portable Document Format)
ISBN 9781503851603 (Online Multi-user eBook)
LCCN 2021939635

Printed in the United States of America

Table of Contents

CHAPTER ONE

Rising from the Grave...4

CHAPTER TWO

History of Vampires...8

CHAPTER THREE

Drinking Blood...14

CHAPTER FOUR

Vampires Today...18

Glossary...22

To Learn More...23

Index...24

CHAPTER ONE
RISING FROM THE GRAVE

Two girls walked on a gravel path. They came to an old cemetery in Exeter, Rhode Island. They decided to explore. The afternoon sunlight shone on the gray headstones. Some were crumbling. Others had vines growing on them.

One of the girls stopped at a grave marked for Mercy L. She told her friend the story of Mercy Lena Brown. Mercy died in 1892 of **tuberculosis**. Her mother and sister had died before her. At that time, people did not understand tuberculosis. The disease seemed to drain the life out of people.

Many towns in the northeastern United States had vampire scares in the 1800s.

When Mercy's brother fell ill after her death, a neighbor suggested that one of his sisters was a vampire. Vampires are undead creatures. They rise from the grave and suck people's blood. People thought a vampire was stealing the life from Mercy's brother.

In the past, people sometimes dug up bodies to make sure a dead person had not become a vampire.

Townspeople told the father to dig up the bodies and check for blood as evidence. Mercy's heart still had blood in it. This made some people believe she was a vampire. They did not know that blood remains in some **organs** after death.

The girls paused quietly when the story was over. Then they turned to walk back home. They wondered how vampire legends got started.

CHAPTER TWO
HISTORY OF VAMPIRES

Modern-day vampire legends began in Europe. They were based on misunderstandings about what happens to bodies when people die. Bodies break down. Soft parts such as skin, hair, and organs shrink and **decompose**. This can make it look like the teeth are growing longer. Dark fluids from organs may leak out of the mouth. People thought it was blood. They did not know how it got there. They thought dead people could rise from the grave. People thought the dead were drinking living people's blood.

Records from the 1500s show a skeleton buried with a brick in its mouth. People sometimes used to put hard objects in a body's mouth to prevent the person from leaving the grave as a vampire.

Vampire legends say the creatures can rise from the grave.

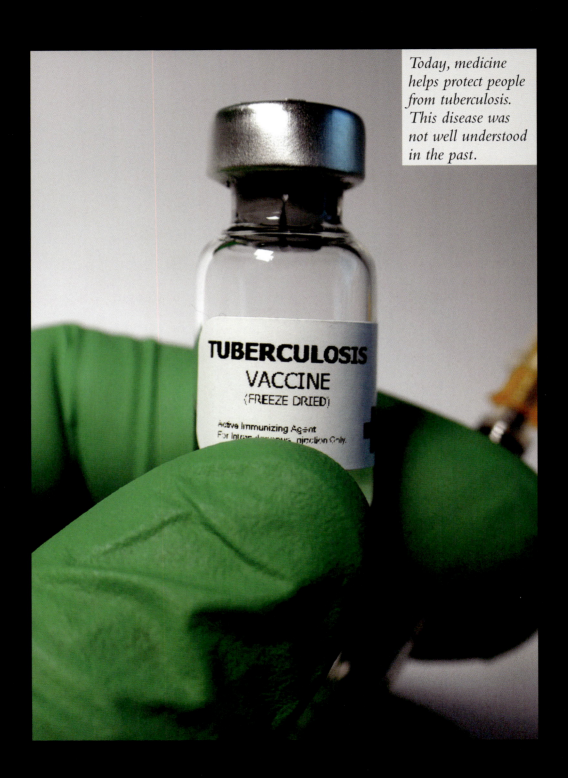

Today, medicine helps protect people from tuberculosis. This disease was not well understood in the past.

Vampire stories were also **inspired** by severe illnesses. People did not know how diseases worked. So they made up vampire stories to explain them. From the mid-1300s, the Black **Plague** spread across Europe. Millions of people died rapidly. The disease caused bleeding mouth sores. Uneducated people thought the sores were signs of being a vampire.

Later, another fast-spreading illness worried many people. Tuberculosis causes people to lose weight. Their skin turns pale. Sometimes they cough up blood. The **symptoms** of this disease looked like evidence of a vampire sucking away life.

Porphyria (por-FEER-ee-uh) is another illness that people connected to vampires. Porphyria causes **sensitivity** to sunlight and reddish-brown teeth. This illness can be passed from parents to children.

Many legends of vampires started in Transylvania, part of modern-day Romania. These legends spread to other parts of the world after disease outbreaks. In Europe, vampire legends became popular in the 1700s. Newspapers told of bodies that had been dug up. The bodies had blood around their mouths.

Then the legends spread around the world. In the 1800s, belief in vampires rose in the United States due to illnesses such as tuberculosis.

Legends of vampire-like creatures exist in many cultures. In the Philippines, they are *manananggal*. They are *peuchen* in Chile and *Baobhan Sith* in Scotland. Australian Aboriginal people call them *Yara-ma-yha-who*. An evil Chinese spirt called *jiangshi* would attack people and drain their energy.

Jiangshi means "stiff corpse." These creatures are also called Chinese hopping vampires.

CHAPTER THREE

DRINKING BLOOD

A vampire's most famous physical feature is long or sharp teeth. Sometimes people call them fangs. Otherwise, the creatures are humanlike. Having human bodies, faces, and voices makes vampires dangerous. They are said to blend in with human crowds. Some stories describe vampires as beautiful. Beauty helps them **lure** people in. Once a vampire gets close to someone, it can attack.

Vampire behavior includes drinking blood. Blood gives vampires life. This means they don't die completely. Sometimes drinking blood kills the victim. Sometimes it turns the victim into a vampire, too.

pale skin

human features

sharp fangs

cold body

In stories around the world, vampires look similar to humans. The main differences are sharp fangs and signs of death, such as pale skin or cold bodies.

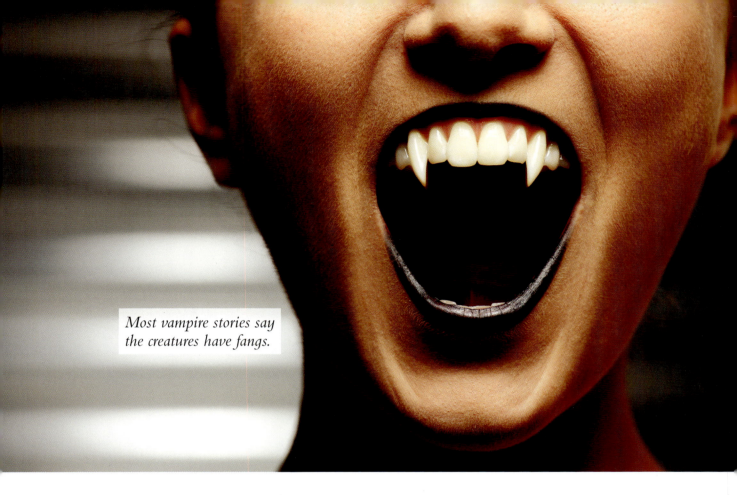

Most vampire stories say the creatures have fangs.

Many legends tell of vampires rising from the grave. Their bodies are cold and pale. They often hunt at night. Sometimes vampires have superstrength. Others can turn into bats. Some do not have shadows and cannot be seen in mirrors or photographs. They might live for hundreds or thousands of years. These features separate vampires from humans.

Humans can defeat vampires. Some stories say vampires do not like garlic. Other stories say they burn quickly in fire. People can kill a vampire by stabbing its heart. Eastern European folklore told of another protection. Stories said vampires liked to count. Someone could spread many seeds in front of a vampire. It would stop to count the seeds. Then the person could escape.

Some stories say garlic and religious symbols, such as crosses, can stop vampires.

CHAPTER FOUR
VAMPIRES TODAY

Vampire legends are where vampire bats got their name. These bats share several characteristics with vampires. They sleep during the day and hunt at night. They feed on blood to survive, and they have pointy teeth.

Bram Stoker wrote the book *Dracula* in 1897. It became very popular and was eventually translated into 44 languages. Over time, millions of copies were sold. The book was about a Transylvanian vampire who drank people's blood. It inspired many books, movies, and shows. Stoker also set the foundation for how vampires would look in later stories. His Count Dracula had pale skin and dark hair.

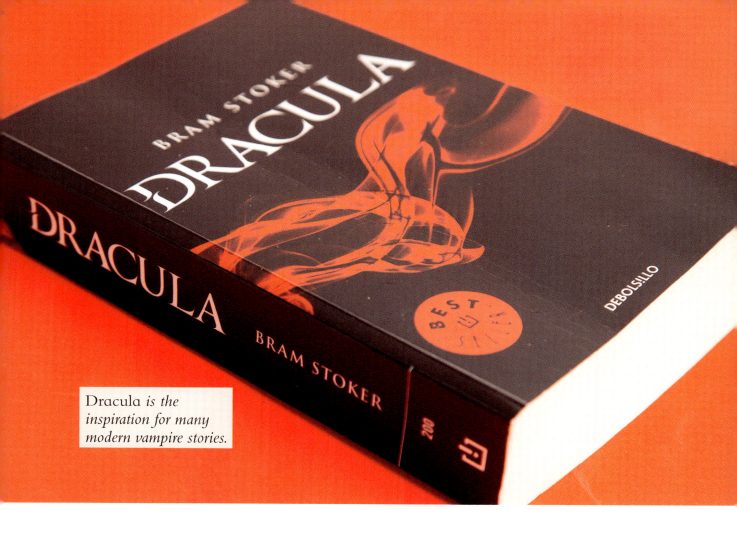

Dracula *is the inspiration for many modern vampire stories.*

Stoker may have named his character Dracula because of a real person. Vlad the Impaler was a prince in the 1400s. He ruled in Wallachia, or modern-day Romania. He was a harsh ruler known for killing his enemies in bloody ways. He was a knight and was sometimes called *Drăculea*, which later became *Dracula*.

The 1922 horror movie *Nosferatu* first showed vampires being sensitive to sunlight. It was based on Stoker's book and became the first famous vampire movie. The main character was a vampire named Count Orlok. The film *Dracula* was released in 1931. An actor named Bela Lugosi played Count Dracula. He made the character elegant and handsome. Many features of Lugosi's Dracula are included in vampire stories today.

The actor Max Schreck played Count Orlok in Nosferatu.

Bela Lugosi played Count Dracula in the 1931 film.

Vampire legends continued to provide entertainment. *Buffy the Vampire Slayer* was a hit TV show in the late 1990s and early 2000s. It was about a girl named Buffy who fought vampires and other monsters. Today, some people actually claim to be vampires. Vampires have inspired tales around the world for centuries.

GLOSSARY

decompose (dee-kuhm-POZE) To decompose is to break down over time. When living things die, they decompose.

inspired (in-SPIYRD) To have inspired something is to have influenced or brought about something else. Vampire legends inspired the name for vampire bats.

lure (LOOR) To lure is to draw close. In some legends, vampires lure people in with their beauty.

organs (OR-gunz) Organs are body parts, such as the heart and lungs. Blood flows through organs.

plague (PLAYG) A plague is a deadly disease outbreak. The Black Plague increased people's fears about vampires.

sensitivity (sen-si-TIV-ih-tee) Sensitivity is being easily hurt or damaged. Vampires hunt at night because of their sensitivity to light.

symptoms (SIMP-tuhms) Symptoms are signs of sickness. Symptoms of tuberculosis are coughing up blood, having pale skin, and losing weight.

tuberculosis (too-bur-kyoo-LOH-sis) Tuberculosis is a disease that attacks a person's lungs. Tuberculosis is one illness that inspired some vampire legends.

TO LEARN MORE

In the Library

Lassieur, Allison. *Scary Stuff.* Mankato, MN: The Child's World, 2021.

Marsico, Katie. *Undead Monsters: From Mummies to Zombies.* Minneapolis, MN: Lerner, 2016.

Mason, Jennifer. *Vampire Myths.* New York, NY: Gareth Stevens Publishing, 2018.

On the Web

Visit our website for links about vampires:

childsworld.com/links

Note to Parents, Teachers, and Librarians: We routinely verify our Web links to make sure they are safe and active sites. So encourage your readers to check them out!

INDEX

appearance, 14–16, 18, 20

bats, 16, 18
Black Plague, 11
blood, 5–6, 8, 11, 12, 14, 18–19
bodies after death, 6, 8
Brown, Mercy Lena, 4–6
Buffy the Vampire Slayer, 21

defeating vampires, 17
Dracula, 18–20

Nosferatu, 20

Romania, 12, 18–19

teeth, 8, 11, 14, 18
tuberculosis, 4–6, 11, 13

ABOUT THE AUTHOR

Emma Huddleston lives in Minnesota with her husband. She enjoys running, swing dancing, and writing books for young readers. She thinks legends about creatures are fascinating!